# Once Upon a Time in X-Blocks® Land

## Nine Magical Quilt Designs

BY PATRICIA PEPE
with Rebecca True

REV 1 - September 2009 Reprint

# Dedication

to my dear mother Margaret
who gave me time to play and freedom to be creative


# Acknowledgements

I WANT TO THANK

Most importantly, my Lord and Savior Jesus Christ,
who gives His gifts so abundantly-

My husband Alan for encouraging me to take the BIG step
and making the journey an adventure

My children:
Arielle, for her energy, enthusiasm and assistance with everything
Michelle and Bear
for hanging in there through all the bumps in the road
and helping out whenever you were needed.

Special thanks to my dear friend Rebecca True for all the beautiful quilts she made for this book and
her inspiration, motivation and unwavering belief in the X-Blocks miracle.
I treasure our friendship.

To the princess Andrea Macy for her continual assistance with all the loose ends that
need tying and her countless hours of "administrative assistance"

Jeanne Poe for always being ready to jump in and lend a hand–

All my girlfriends in the Ladies of the Evening quilt group for their support and encouragement
from the very beginning - I couldn't have made it without you gals!

Cheryl & Gary Phillips of Phillips Fiber Arts for their willingness
to share their knowledge and friendship – Bless you two!

Robin Black at Blackbird Creative for her patience and willingness to see this project through

Lisa Marie Browning for making my cover illustration come to life and all the interior artwork

Dennis Swanson of Studio 101 West for photography of the quilts

And last but certainly not least -
Gloria, Steve and Tara at Palmer Printing for catching my vision -
their tremendous creativity and assistance with all the many details
helped make my dream come true!





ISBN: 978-0-9815172-0-9

# Contents

## BINDING

The binding used for the projects in this book are made with 2¼" wide straight grain strips, cut across the width of the fabric.

1. Cut the specified number of strips for your project and sew them together, end-to-end using a diagonal seam, to make one continuous strip. Trim the seam to ¼" and press open.
2. Fold and press the binding in half lengthwise with wrong sides together.
3. Starting in the center of one side of the quilt, place binding strip on right side of quilt top, raw edges even; leaving a 10" tail.
4. Sew binding to quilt top, mitering corners. Stop approximately 20" from where you started.
5. Remove quilt from sewing machine and lay on a flat surface. Place the tail of the first binding end in place on edge of quilt top. Repeat with second tail. Make a crease in the second tail where it meets the end of the first tail. Measure 2¼" from the crease and cut the second tail straight across at that mark.
6. Open both tails and place right sides together at a right angle. Sew a diagonal seam, trim to ¼" and press open. Re-fold binding strip in half lengthwise and finish stitching to edge of quilt top.
7. Fold binding over edge of quilt, hiding seam and hand stitch securely in place with invisible stitch.

## Helpful Hints From the Queen

- Before using your X-Blocks tool, remove the protective backing. Placing non-slip disks or film on both sides of the tool will help prevent movement when cutting with the rotary cutter.
- 100% cotton or other natural fiber fabrics are recommended.
- Use a generous ¼" seam allowance, unless instructed otherwise.
- Use the full width of the fabric (42"- 44") when cutting strips, unless individual quilt directions state otherwise.
- Stripe fabrics work exceptionally well for X-Blocks. Different designs will emerge depending on where the stripe is placed in the original block.

Some designs require the X-Blocks to be flipped over before cutting. Double check the placement of the X-Blocks tool before cutting each time.

## FUSIBLE WEB APPLIQUE

Using your favorite paper backed fusible web product, these easy steps will help you create the applique shapes in the My Little Princess quilt.

1. With a pencil, trace each shape onto the paper side of the fusible web, as many times as needed, using the pattern provided in project.
2. Following the manufacturer's instructions, fuse the drawn shapes to the wrong side of the chosen appliqué fabric. Let cool and then cut out each appliqué shape on the drawn line.
3. Remove the paper backing from the shapes and position them on the background fabric, referring to diagram for placement. Fuse the shapes in place.
4. Machine stitch around the edges of each shape with matching thread to secure the edges and prevent fraying. You could also use a decorative stitch such as a blanket or zigzag stitch for a different look.

# 1+1+1=Fun!

## Strips of fabric create your designs

Wish Upon a Star

Prints Charming

Sleeping Beauty

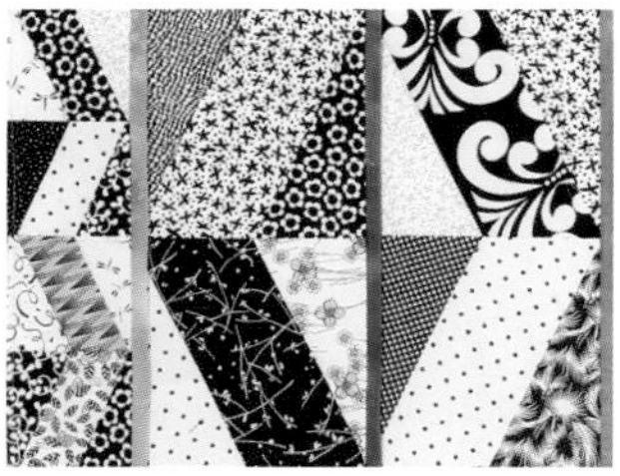

Knight Time

# Wish Upon A Star

***...Those who wish to sing always find a song.***

Quilt made by Andrea Macy

# Materials

Yardages are based on 42"- wide fabrics

| Finished quilt size: | 51" x 51" | 45" x 45" | Approx. 26" x 26" | Approx. 24" x 24" |
|---|---|---|---|---|
| | **7½" X-Blocks** | **6½" X-Blocks** | **Mini-7.5 Mini-6.5 X-Blocks** | **Bellybutton-7.5 Bellybutton-6.5 X-Blocks** |
| Blue print for blocks & outer border | 1⅓ yds. | 1¼ yds. | ½ yd. | ⅓ yd. |
| Red print for blocks & outer border | 1⅓ yds. | 1¼ yds. | ½ yd. | ⅓ yd. |
| Yellow/multi color print for blocks, inner border, binding | 2 yds. | 1½ yds. | ¾ yd. | ½ yd. |
| Backing fabric | 3 yds. | 2½ yds. | 1 yd. | 1 yd. |

# Cutting Chart

Cut all strips across the width of the fabric (WOF) - 42"- 44"

| | **7½" X-Blocks** | **6½" X-Blocks** | **Mini-7.5 X-Blocks** | **Mini-6.5 X-Blocks** | **Bellybutton-7.5 X-Blocks** | **Bellybutton-6.5 X-Blocks** |
|---|---|---|---|---|---|---|
| Blue print | 9 strips -3¾" | 8 strips - 3¼" | 6 strips - 2⅛" | 5 strips - 1⅞" | 5 strips - 2" | 5 strips -1¾" |
| Outer border | 2 strips - 4" | 2 strips - 4" | 1 strip - 2½" | 1 strip - 2½" | 1 strip - 2½" | 1 strip - 2½" |
| Red print | 9 strips - 3¾" | 8 strips - 3¼" | 6 strips - 2⅛" | 5 strips - 1⅞" | 5 strips - 2" | 5 strips - 1¾" |
| Outer border | 2 strips - 4" | 2 strips - 4" | 1 strip - 2½" | 1 strip - 2½" | 1 strip - 2½" | 1 strip - 2½" |
| Yellow/multi color print | 9 strips - 3¾" | 8 strips - 3¼" | 6 strips - 2⅛" | 5 strips - 1⅞" | 5 strips - 2" | 5 strips - 1¾" |
| Inner border | 5 strips - 1½" | 4 strips - 1½" | 2 strips - 1¼" | 1 strip - 2½" | 1 strip - 2½" | 1 strip - 2½" |
| Binding | 6 strips - 2¼" | 5 strips - 2¼" | 3 strips - 2" | 3 strips - 2" | 3 strips - 2" | 3 strips - 2" |

# Wish Upon a Star

## MAKING THE BLOCKS

Sew a blue strip between a red and yellow strip along long edges to make strip set. Repeat with all strips. Press seams to the center strip with light spray starch.

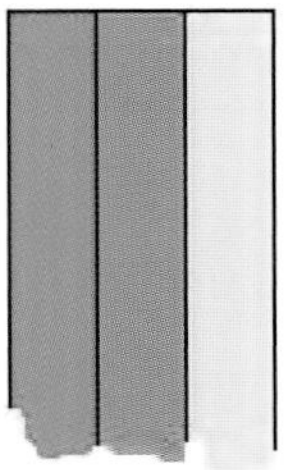

Place X-Blocks tool on top of strip set, matching solid lines to the seams of the strip set. You will only need to match the vertical lines of the tool.

Cut around the edges of the X-Blocks with a rotary cutter, setting aside the X-tra's for your border.

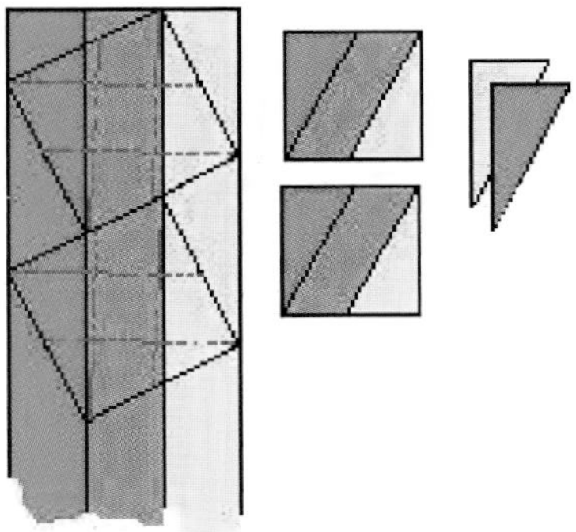

Continue moving the X-Blocks down the strip set, lining up the seams to the lines on the tool to cut a total of 36 blocks. After your blocks are cut, handle them gently as the edges are bias and will stretch if not careful. They are perfectly square and ready to sew into your quilt top.

Referring to the quilt diagram, sew groups of four blocks together, turning each block a quarter turn, placing the yellow corners of each block together to create stars. Press seams to either side. Repeat with all blocks to create nine stars.

Sew the nine stars together in three rows of three stars each, matching seams. Press seams in opposite directions, pressing open when necessary to minimize bulk. Sew the inner border strips together end-to-end to make continuous strip. Sew to all sides of quilt top; press to border strips.

## MAKING THE X-TRA'S BORDER

Sew together 16 red X-tra's with 16 yellow/multi X-tra's as shown to make rectangles. Trim all rectangles so they are equal in size. (The size of the rectangle will vary, depending on size of X-Blocks tool, individual seam allowance, etc.) Sew 4 rectangles together end-to-end to make strip, joining the red end of one rectangle to the red end of the next.

*Repeat with 4 more rectangles.*

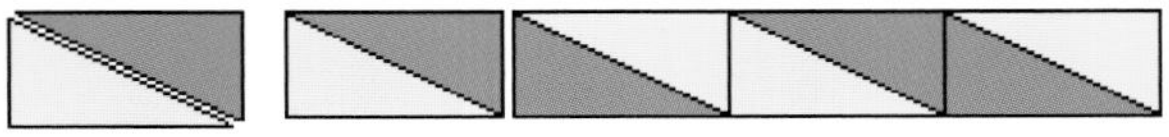

Trim red and blue border strips to same width as pieced rectangles. Measure one side of the quilt top. Add a red border strip to one of the 4-rectangle strips to fit this measurement. Sew to side. Press seam to border. Measure the adjoining side of the quilt top, including the border you just added. Sew another red border strip to a 4-rectangle strip to fit this measurement. Sew to side. Press seam to border. Repeat for last two sides of quilt top, using the blue border strips in place of the red.

### Magic Rotary Cutter Wand TIP

It is helpful to use a light spray starch when pressing. Once your blocks are cut you will want to handle them gently since the edges are bias and will stretch if not treated carefully. If the blocks do get slightly stretched, they can be re-cut using the X-Blocks tool as before.

# Wish Upon a Star

### FINISHING THE QUILT

Refer to "Happy Endings" on page 8 to layer and baste your quilt, and quilt as desired. Prepare binding and sew to the quilted top.

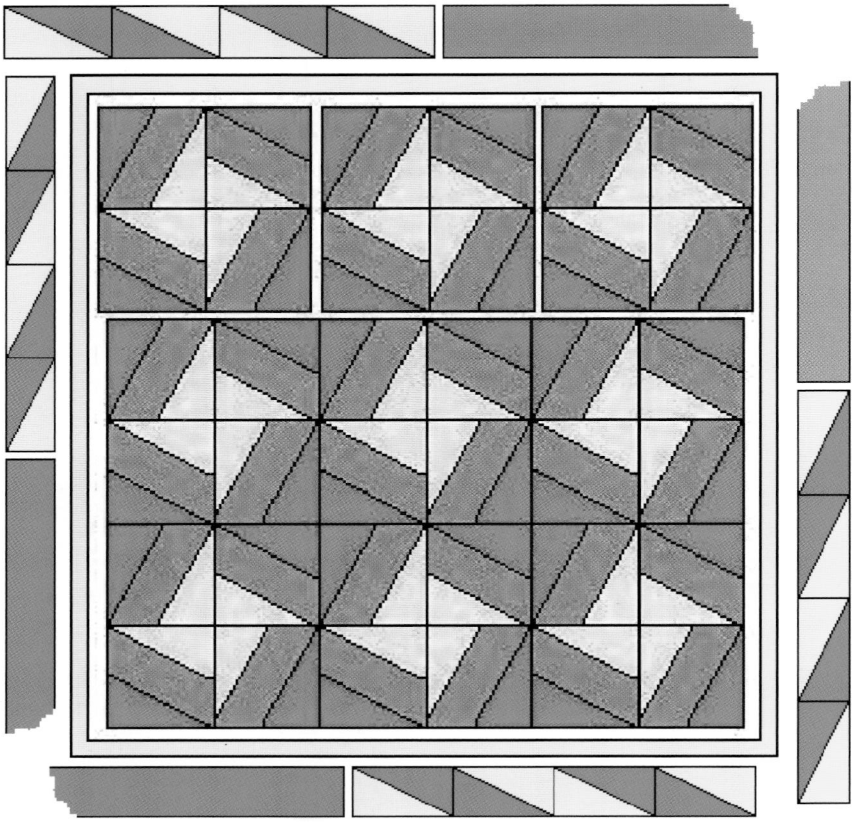

*Quilt Assembly*

# Prints Charming

***...He will be called Prince of Peace.***
*Isaiah 9:6*

Quilt made by Patricia Pepe

# Materials

Yardages are based on 42"- wide fabrics

| Finished quilt size: | 57" x 78" | 50" x 68" | Approx. 33 x 41" | Approx. 28" x 36" | Approx. 30" x 38" | Approx. 26" x 34" |
|---|---|---|---|---|---|---|
| | **7½" X-Blocks** | **6½" X-Blocks** | **Mini-7.5** | **Mini-6.5** | **Bellybutton-7.5** | **Bellybutton-6.5** |
| Dark aqua-blue print | 1⅔ yds. | 1¼ yds. | ¾ yd. | ½ yd. | ½ yd. | ½ yd. |
| Assorted gold & aqua prints | 4½ yds. | 3¼ yds. | 1½ yds. | 1½ yds. | 1½ yds. | 1½ yds. |
| Aqua print for inner border & binding | 1⅛ yds. | 1 yd. | ¾ yd. | ¾ yd. | ¾ yd. | ¾ yd. |
| Backing | 3¼ yd. | 3 yds. | 1½ yd. | 1 yd. | 1 yd. | 1 yd. |

# Cutting Chart

Cut all strips across the width of the fabric (WOF) - 42"- 44"

| | **7½" X-Blocks** | **6½" X-Blocks** | **Mini-7.5 X-Blocks** | **Mini-6.5 X-Blocks** | **Bellybutton - 7.5 X-Blocks** | **Bellybutton - 6.5 X-Blocks** |
|---|---|---|---|---|---|---|
| Dark aqua-blue print | 18 strips - 2¾" | 14 strips - 2⅜" | 10 strips - 1½" | 9 strips - 1⅜" | 9 strips - 1½" | 9 strips - 1¼" |
| Sub-cut strips into 70 rectangles | 10¼" | 9" | 5½" | 5" | 5¼" | 4½" |
| Assorted gold & aqua prints | 36 strips - 4¼" | 28 strips - 3⅞" | 20 strips - 2½" | 18 strips - 2¼" | 18 strips - 2⅜" | 18 strips - 2⅛" |
| Sub-cut strips into 140 rectangles | 10¼" | 9" | 5½" | 5" | 5¼" | 4½" |
| Aqua print for inner border | 6 strips - 2½" | 6 strips - 2½" | 4 strips - 2" | 4 strips - 1¾" | 4 strips - 1¾" | 4 strips - 1½" |
| Binding | 7 strips 2¼" | 6 strips 2¼" | 4 strips 2¼" | 4 strips 2¼" | 4 strips 2¼" | 4 strips 2¼" |

# Prints Charming

## MAKING THE BLOCKS

Sew a dark aqua-blue strip between two assorted gold or aqua print strips on the long edges to make a block. Repeat with all strips to make 70 blocks, keeping the dark aqua print in the center and mixing the gold and aqua prints for each block. Press seams toward the center strip with a light spray starch.

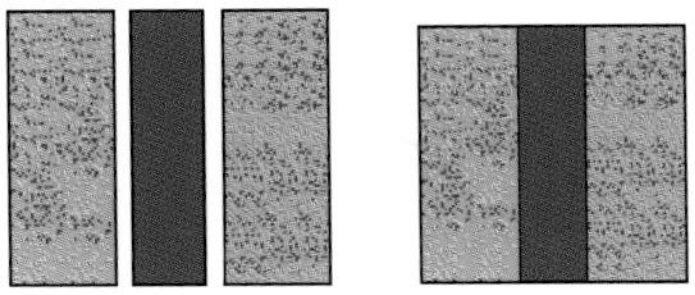

Place the X-Blocks tool on top of a block, matching dotted lines of tool to the seams of the block. You will only need to match the vertical lines of the tool.

Cut around the edges of the X-Blocks with a rotary cutter, setting aside the X-tra's for your border. Repeat with all 70 blocks.

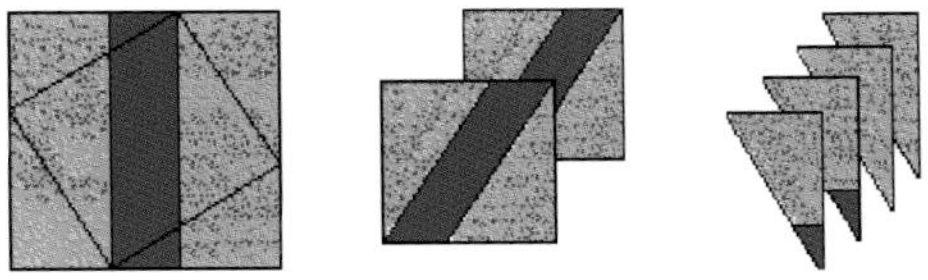

After your blocks are cut, handle them gently as the edges are bias and will stretch if not careful. They are perfectly square and ready to sew into your quilt top.

## QUILT TOP ASSEMBLY

Referring to the quilt assembly diagram, arrange the blocks into 10 horizontal rows of 7 blocks each, rotating the blocks as needed to distribute the colors and create a pleasing arrangement. Sew the blocks into rows. Press the seam allowances in opposite directions from row to row. Sew the rows together, pressing the seam allowances in either direction or open when necessary to minimize bulk.

Sew the inner border strips together end to end and press the seams to one side. Refer to "Happy Endings" on page 8 to cut and sew the borders.

## MAKING THE X-TRA'S BORDER

Sew X-tra's together as shown to make a rectangle. Repeat with all X-tra's. Trim all rectangles to an equal size. (The size of the rectangle will vary, depending on size of X-Blocks tool, individual seam allowance, etc.)

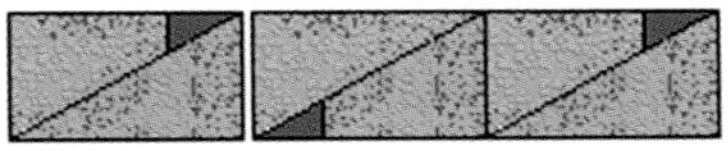

Measure the sides of the quilt top. Sew rectangles together end-to-end to fit this measurement. Sew X-tra's border to sides of quilt, press seams to the quilt top.

Measure quilt through the center from side to side, including borders you just added. Sew X-tra's rectangles together to fit this measurement and sew to the top and bottom edges of your quilt top. Press seams to the quilt top. Edge stitch 1/8" around the outer edge of X-tra's border to prevent seams from pulling out.

# Prints Charming

## FINISHING THE QUILT

Refer to "Happy Endings" on page 8 to layer and baste your quilt, and quilt as desired. Prepare binding and sew to the quilted top.

*Quilt Assembly*

# Sleeping Beauty

*...There's nothing better under heaven above, than sleeping under a quilt made with love.*

Quilt made by Patricia Pepe

# Materials

Yardages are based on 42"- wide fabrics

| Finished quilt size: | 52" x 66" | 46" x 58" | 27" x 34" - 24" x 30" | 26" x 32" - 22" x 28" |
|---|---|---|---|---|
| | **7½" X-Blocks** | **6½" X-Blocks** | **Mini-7.5 Mini-6.5 X-Blocks** | **Bellybutton-7.5 Bellybutton-6.5 X-Blocks** |
| Green floral | 1¾ yds. | 1½ yds. | ⅔ yd. | ⅔ yd. |
| Cream floral | 2 yds. | 1¾ yds. | ¾ yd. | ¾ yd. |
| Rose | 1⅓ yds. | 1⅓ yds. | ⅔ yd. | ⅔ yd. |
| Binding | ¾ yd. | ½ yd. | ⅓ yd. | ⅓ yd. |
| Backing fabric | 3½ yds. | 3 yds. | 1 yd. | 1 yd. |

# Cutting Chart

Cut all strips across the width of the fabric (WOF) - 42"- 44"

| | **7½" X-Blocks** | **6½" X-Blocks** | **Mini-7.5 X-Blocks** | **Mini-6.5 X-Blocks** | **Bellybutton-7.5 X-Blocks** | **Bellybutton-6.5 X-Blocks** |
|---|---|---|---|---|---|---|
| Green floral | 12 strips - 4¼" | 12 strips - 4" | 7 strips - 2½" | 7 strips - 2¼" | 7 strips - 2½" | 7 strips - 2¼" |
| Cream floral<br>Inner border #2 | 12 strips - 4¼"<br>5 strips - 1¾" | 12 strips - 4"<br>5 strips - 1¾" | 7 strips - 2½"<br>4 strips - 1¼" | 7 strips - 2¼"<br>4 strips - 1¼" | 7 strips - 2½"<br>4 strips - 1¼" | 7 strips - 2¼"<br>4 strips - 1¼" |
| Rose<br>Inner border #1 | 12 strips -2¾"<br>5 strips - 1½" | 12 strips - 2⅜"<br>5 strips - 1½" | 7 strips - 1½"<br>4 strips - 1" | 7 strips - 1⅜"<br>4 strips - 1" | 7 strips - 1½"<br>4 strips - 1" | 7 strips - 1¼"<br>4 strips - 1" |
| Binding | 7 strips - 2¼" | 6 strips - 2¼" | 4 strips - 2¼" | 4 strips - 2¼" | 4 strips - 2¼" | 4 strips - 2¼" |

# Sleeping Beauty

### MAKING THE BLOCKS

Sew a rose strip between green and cream floral strips on long edges to make strip set. Repeat with all strips. Press seams to the center strip with light spray starch.

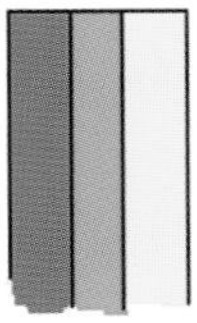

### BASIC X-BLOCKS

Place X-Blocks tool on top of a strip set, matching dotted lines to the seams of the strip set.

Cut around the edges of the X-Blocks with rotary cutter, setting aside the X-tra's for your border. Continue moving the X-Blocks down the strip set, lining up the seams to the lines on the tool to cut a total of 24 blocks.

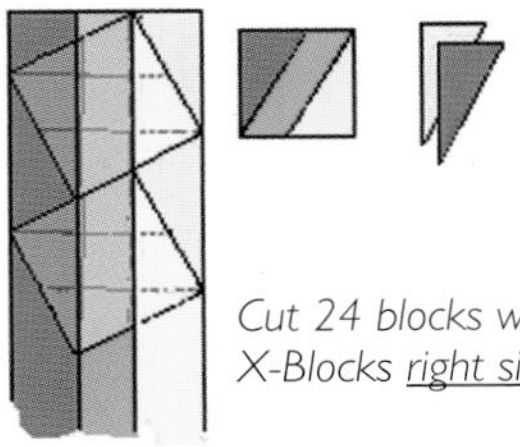

*Cut 24 blocks with X-Blocks right side up*

### REVERSE X-BLOCKS:

Flip the X-Blocks tool over (the printed words on the tool will appear backward) and place on the strip set, again placing lines of tool to seams on strips. Cut around the edges of the X-Blocks with rotary cutter, setting aside the X-tra's for your border. Continue moving the X-Blocks down the strip set, lining up the seams to the lines on the tool to cut a total of 24 reverse blocks.

After all of your blocks are cut, handle them gently as the edges are bias and will stretch if not careful. They are perfectly square and ready to sew into your quilt top.

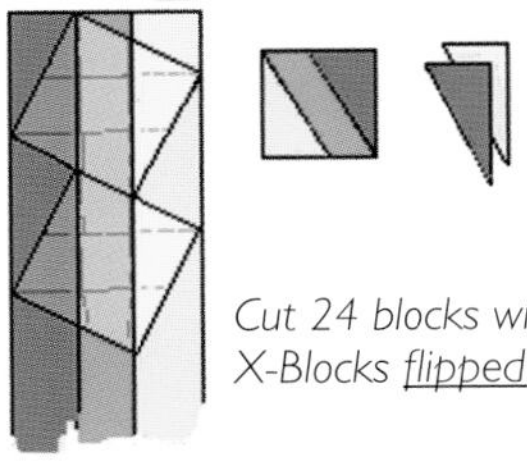

*Cut 24 blocks with X-Blocks flipped over*

Referring to the quilt diagram, sew groups of four blocks together, 2 each basic and reverse blocks, turning each block a quarter turn, placing the green floral fabric together to create diamonds. (This will automatically create the cream floral diamonds). Press seams to either side. Repeat with all blocks to create twelve diamonds.

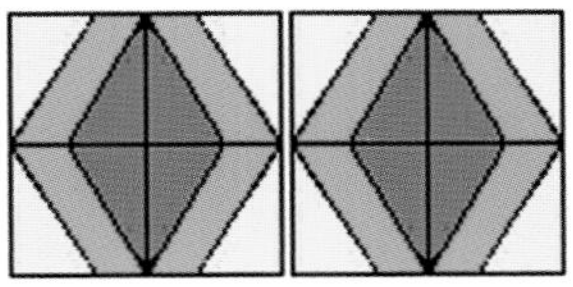

Sew diamond blocks together into 4 rows of 3 diamonds each, following diagram. Press seams in opposite directions from row to row. Sew rows together pressing seams in either direction or open to minimize bulk.

Sew the inner border strips together end to end and press seam allowances to one side. Measure the quilt through the center from top to bottom and cut two inner border strips to that measurement. Sew to sides of quilt, press seams to quilt top. Repeat to add inner borders to top and bottom of quilt. Repeat for inner border #2.

**Magic Rotary Cutter Wand TIP**

**To save even more time and fabric, sew your strips together end-to-end before sewing into the strip sets. This will create a seam in some of your blocks, but it's almost impossible to see once it's quilted!**

# Sleeping Beauty

### MAKING THE X-TRA'S BORDER

Sew Basic X-tra's together as shown, then end-to-end to make strip. Repeat with Reverse X-tra's.

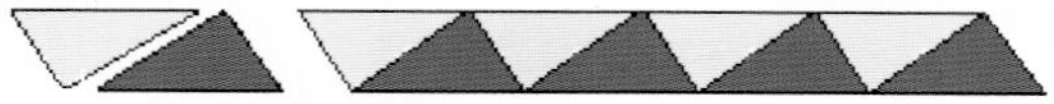

*X-tra's from Basic X-Blocks*

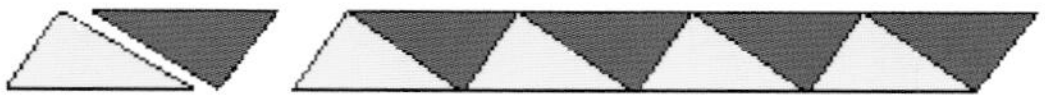

*X-tra's from Reverse X-Blocks*

Measure the quilt through the center from top to bottom and cut two X-tra's border strips to that measurement. Sew to sides of quilt, press seams to inner border. Measure the quilt through the center from side to side and cut two X-tra's border strips to that measurement. Sew to top and bottom of quilt, press seams to inner border.

### FINISHING THE QUILT

Refer to "Happy Endings" on page 8 to layer and baste your quilt, and quilt as desired. Prepare binding and sew to the quilted top.

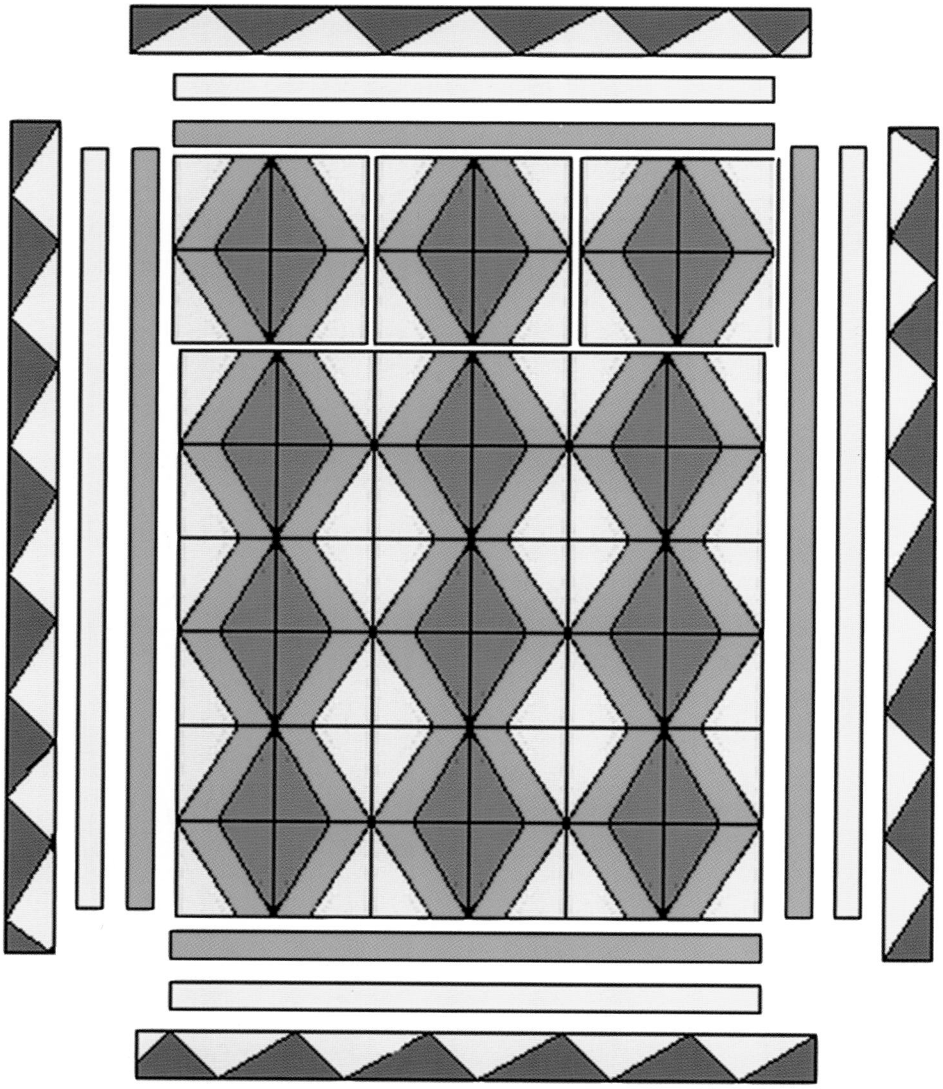

*Quilt Assembly*

# Pieceful Palace

## 9-patch blocks create your designs

Once Upon a Dream

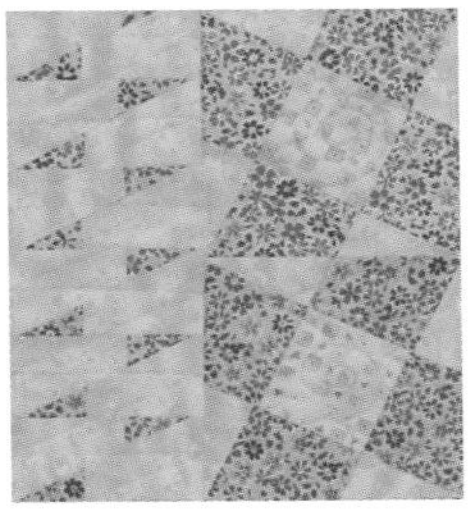

My Little Princess

Happily Ever Laughter

# Walk Around the Blocks Gallery

Quilt made by Emma Woods

12 year old X-Blocks adventurer Emma Woods from Ventura, CA created this striking variation of Wish Upon a Star. Way to go Emma!

Quilts made by Shirley Handlang

Shirley Handlang of Ballwin, MO calls these her 'lemonade' quilts because she used nine-patch blocks she had received in a block exchange. What a stunning transformation! Shirley certainly made some sweet lemonade!

Quilt made by Morgan Pepe

When she was 17 years old, my niece Morgan Pepe from Atascadero, CA made this sophisticated variation of Sleeping Beauty for her mother. Lucky mom!

Quilt made by Frieda Lowe

My dear friend, Frieda Lowe of Paradise, CA made this lovely variation of Crown Jewels in a variety of rich red and tan prints. Simply beautiful!

Quilt designed by Sara Silver

This fabulous X-Blocks quilt is an original design created by Sara Silver of Scottsdale, AZ using the Moda Marbles collection. Wow!

# Once Upon A Dream

***...Sweet dreams, sleep tight;***
***God loves you and good night.***

Quilts made by Patricia Pepe
Quilted by Peggy Hasch

# Materials

Yardages are based on 42"- wide fabrics

| Finished quilt size: | 49" x 63" | 42" x 54" | Approx. 27" x 34" | Approx. 26" x 34" |
|---|---|---|---|---|
| | **7½" X-Blocks** | **6½" X-Blocks** | **Mini-7.5<br>Mini-6.5<br>X-Blocks** | **Bellybutton-7.5<br>Bellybutton-6.5<br>X-Blocks** |
| 7 assorted light blue or pink prints | ¼ yd. each print (1¾ yd. total) | ¼ yd. each print (1¾ yd. total) | ¼ yd. each print (⅞ yd. total) | ¼ yd. each print (⅞ yd. total) |
| Brown print | 2 yds. | 1½ yds. | ¾ yd. | ⅔ yd. |
| Blue or pink print for inner border & binding | 1 yd. | ¾ yds. | ½ yd. | ½ yd. |
| Blue or pink print for outer border | 1 yd. | ¾ yd. | ½ yd. | ½ yd. |
| Backing | 3 yds. | 2½ yds. | 1 yd. | 1 yd. |

# Cutting Chart

Cut all strips across the width of the fabric (WOF) - 42"- 44"

| | **7½" X-Blocks** | **6½" X-Blocks** | **Mini-7.5 X-Blocks** | **Mini-6.5 X-Blocks** | **Bellybutton-7.5 X-Blocks** | **Bellybutton-6.5 X-Blocks** |
|---|---|---|---|---|---|---|
| 7 diff. lt. blue or lt. pink prints<br>Cut 20 squares from each print (total 140) | 2 strips from each print (14 total) 3¾"<br>3¾" x 3¾" | 2 strips from each print (14 total) 3¼"<br>3¼" x 3¼" | 1 strip from each print (14 total) 2⅛"<br>2⅛" x 2⅛" | 1 strip from each print (14 total) 1⅞"<br>1⅞" x 1⅞" | 1 strip from each print (14 total) 2"<br>2" x 2" | 1 strip from each print (14 total) 1¾"<br>1¾" x 1¾" |
| Brown print<br>Sub-cut into 175 squares | 16 strips - 3¾"<br>3¾" x 3¾" | 15 strips - 3¼"<br>3¼" x 3¼" | 10 strips - 2⅛"<br>2⅛" x 2⅛" | 9 strips - 1⅞"<br>1⅞" x 1⅞" | 9 strips - 2"<br>2" x 2" | 8 strips - 1¾"<br>1¾" x 1¾" |
| Inner border | 5 strips - 2½" | 5 strips - 2¼" | 3 strips - 1½" | 3 strips - 1½" | 3 strips - 1½" | 3 strips - 1½" |
| Outer border | 6 strips - 4½" | 5 strips - 4" | 3 strips - 3½" | 3 strips - 3½" | 3 strips - 3½" | 3 strips - 3½" |
| Binding | 6 strips -2¼" | 5 strips -2¼" | 4 strips -2¼" | 4 strips -2¼" | 4 strips -2¼" | 4 strips -2¼" |

# Once Upon A Dream

### MAKING THE BLOCKS

Sew 4 of the same blue or pink print squares and 5 brown squares together as shown to make a nine-patch block. Press seams to the brown fabric. Repeat to make a total of 35 nine-patch blocks – *using one blue/pink print for each nine patch block.* You will have 5 blocks of each of the 7 blue/pink prints. Press all blocks with light starch.

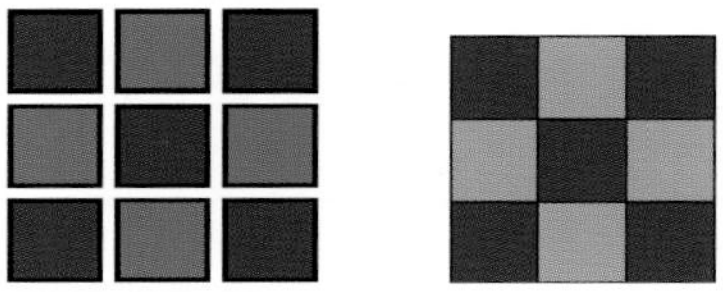

Place X-Blocks tool on a nine-patch block, matching the **solid** lines of the tool to the seams of the X-Blocks tool. Cut along edges of X-Blocks with rotary cutter. Set aside the cut-off wedges (X-tra's) to use for your border. Cut all 35 blocks in this manner. After your blocks are cut, handle them gently as the edges are bias and will stretch if not careful.

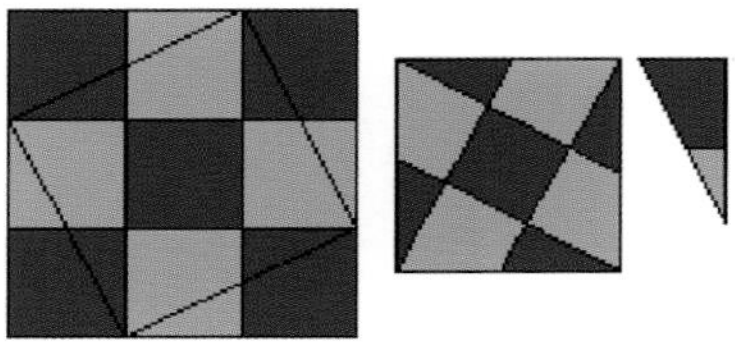

*X-tra's for border*

*Cut along edges with rotary cutter*

*Note: If you are using a Mini or Bellybutton X-Blocks, the cut-off wedges are very small and more difficult to work with so a border of complementary fabric might be used in place of the X-tra's border.*

### ASSEMBLING THE QUILT TOP

Sew the blocks together into 7 rows of 5 blocks each matching seams and ends as shown in quilt assembly diagram. Press the seams in each row in opposite directions. Join the rows. Press seams to either side or open to minimize bulk.

Sew the inner border strips together end to end and press the seams to one side. Sew to all sides of quilt top.

### MAKING THE X-TRA'S BORDER

Sew the X-tra's together as shown to make wedge rectangles. Trim all rectangles to equal size.

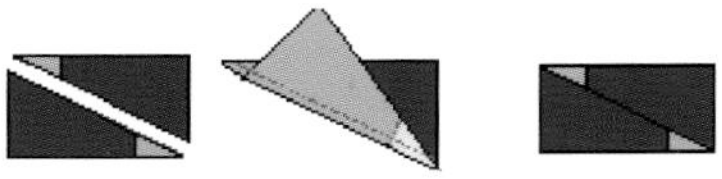

Measure the sides of the quilt top. Sew the rectangles together, end to end as shown to make border strip. Trim the X-tra's border as necessary to fit the measurement of the sides; sew to quilt.

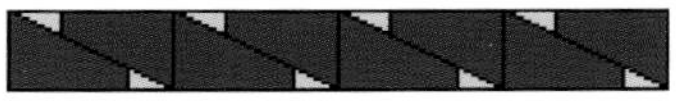

Measure the width of an X-tra's rectangle. Cut 4 squares brown texture the same width as the trimmed X-tra rectangles, set aside.

*Measure width*

Measure the top and bottom edges of quilt top. Sew remaining rectangles together, adding one brown square to each end to fit measurement of top. Sew to top of quilt. Repeat for bottom of quilt. Press seams toward the inner border.

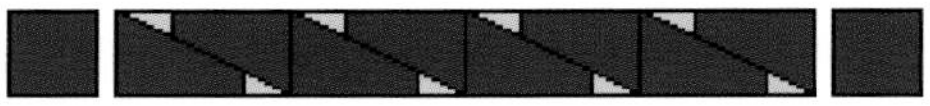

Sew the outer border strips together end to end pressing seams to one side. Refer to "Adding Borders" on page 8 to cut and sew the border.

**Magic Rotary Cutter Wand TIP**

Place your X-tra's in to separate stacks as you cut your blocks, then into zipper top baggies.

# Once Upon A Dream

### FINISHING THE QUILT

Refer to "Happy Endings" on page 8 to layer and baste your quilt. Quilt as desired. Prepare the binding strips and sew to all edges of quilt top.

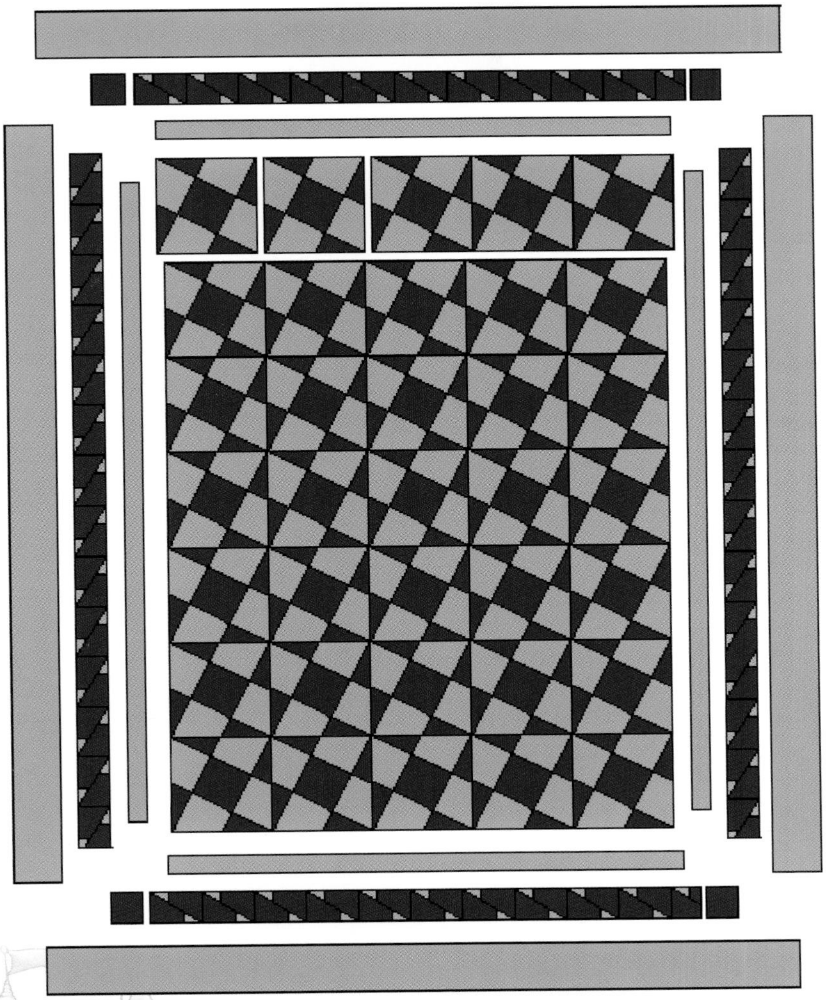

*Quilt Assembly*

# My Little Princess

***...a wee bit of heaven drifted down from above, a handful of happiness and a heart full of love.***

Designed by Arielle Pepe

# Materials - Yardages are based on 42"- wide fabrics

| Finished quilt size: | 74" x 74" | 67" x 67" | Approx. 39" x 39" & 36" x 36" | Approx. 37" x 37" & 34" x 34" |
|---|---|---|---|---|
| | **7½" X-Blocks** | **6½" X-Blocks** | **Mini-7.5 Mini-6.5** | **Bellybutton-7.5 Bellybutton-6.5** |
| Lime green - background & appliqué panel | 3 yds. | 2½ yds. | 1 yd. | 1 yd. |
| Blue floral - blocks & borders | 2½ yds. | 2 yds. | 1 yd. | 1 yd. |
| Pink floral - blocks | 1½ yd. | 2½ yds. | 1 yd. | 1 yd. |
| Light blue print - blue block centers | ½ yd. | ½ yd. | ¼ yd. | ¼ yd. |
| Light pink print - pink block centers | ½ yd. | ½ yd. | ¼ yd. | ¼ yd. |
| Aqua solid - appliqués & panel | ½ yd. | ½ yd. | ¼ yd. | ¼ yd. |
| Medium pink solid - flowers | ⅛ yd. | ⅛ yd. | ⅛ yd. | ⅛ yd. |
| Dark pink solid - flower centers | small scrap | small scrap | small scrap | small scrap |
| Blue solid - dots | small scrap | small scrap | small scrap | small scrap |
| Binding & backing | 5½ yds. | 4½ yds. | 2 yds. | 2 yds. |

# Cutting Chart - Cut all strips across the width of the fabric (WOF) - 42"- 44"

| | **7½" X-Blocks** | **6½" X-Blocks** | **Mini-7.5 X-Blocks** | **Mini-6.5 X-Blocks** | **Bellybutton - 7.5 X-Blocks** | **Bellybutton - 6.5 X-Blocks** |
|---|---|---|---|---|---|---|
| Lime green - Panel (cut first)<br>Background (cut after panel) | 64" x 10½"<br>20 strips - 3¾" | 55" x 9½"<br>18 strips - 3¼" | 33" x 5½"<br>12 strips - 2⅛" | 28" x 5"<br>12 strips - 1⅞" | 30" x 5½"<br>12 strips - 2" | 26" x 5"<br>12 strips - 1¾" |
| Blue floral<br>Outer borders | 11 strips 3¾"<br>8 strips - 5½" | 11 strips 3¼"<br>8 strips - 5½" | 7 strips 2⅛"<br>4 strips - 4" | 7 strips 1⅞"<br>4 strips - 4" | 7 strips 2"<br>4 strips - 4" | 7 strips 1¾"<br>4 strips - 3½" |
| Pink floral | 11 strips 3¾" | 11 strips 3¼" | 7 strips 2⅛" | 7 strips 1⅞" | 7 strips 2" | 7 strips 1¾" |
| Light blue print | 3 strips 3¾" | 3 strips 3¼" | 2 strips 2⅛" | 2 strips 1⅞" | 2 strips 2" | 2 strips 1¾" |
| Light pink print | 3 strips 3¾" | 3 strips 3¼" | 2 strips 2⅛" | 2 strips 1⅞" | 2 strips 2" | 2 strips 1¾" |
| Aqua solid<br>Appliqué | 4 strips 1¼"<br>swirls | 4 strips 1¼"<br>swirls | 2 strips 1"<br>swirls | 2 strips 1"<br>swirls | 2 strips 1"<br>swirls | 2 strips 1"<br>swirls |
| Medium pink solid | flowers | flowers | flowers | flowers | flowers | flowers |
| Dark pink solid | flower centers | flower centers | flower centers | flower centers | flower centers | flower centers |
| Blue solid | dots | dots | dots | dots | dots | dots |
| Binding | 8 strips 2¼" | 7 strips 2¼" | 4 strips 2¼" | 4 strips 2¼" | 4 strips 2¼" | 4 strips 2¼" |

# Segment Cutting Chart - Cut segments after sewing into strip sets per instructions

| | **7½" X-Blocks** | **6½" X-Blocks** | **Mini-7.5 X-Blocks** | **Mini-6.5 X-Blocks** | **Bellybutton - 7.5 X-Blocks** | **Bellybutton - 6.5 X-Blocks** |
|---|---|---|---|---|---|---|
| Strip Sets - A, B, C, & D | 3¾" | 3¼" | 2⅛" | 1⅞" | 2" | 1¾" |

# My Little Princess

### MAKING THE NINE-PATCH BLOCKS

#### Block A

Sew a blue floral strip between two green strips to make strip set A. Press seams to center strip. Sew a light blue strip between two blue floral strips to make strip set B. Press seams to outside strips.

Referring to Segment Cutting Chart for measurement, cut strip set A into 54 segments, cut strip set B into 27 segments.

*Make sure to double check the measurement for the size X-Blocks tool you are using!*

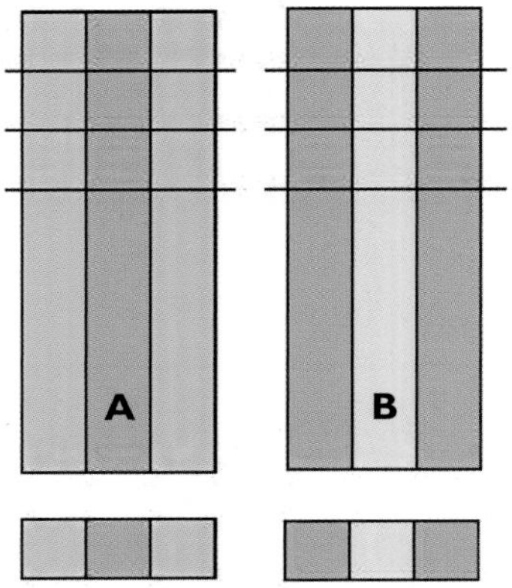


Sew segments together to make a nine-patch block as shown. Press seams to outer segments using a light spray starch. Repeat to make 27 Block A. Set blocks aside.

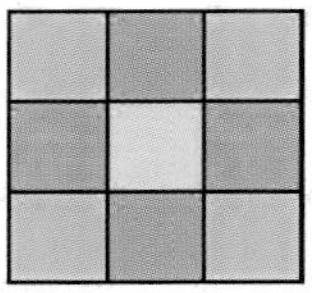

*Block A*

#### Block B:

Sew a pink floral strip between two green strips to make strip set C. Press seams to outer strips. Sew a light pink strip between two pink floral strips to make strip set D. Press seams to floral strips.

Referring to Segment Cutting Chart for measurement, cut strip set C into 54 segments, cut strip set D into 27 segments.

*Make sure to double check the measurement for the size X-Blocks tool you are using!*

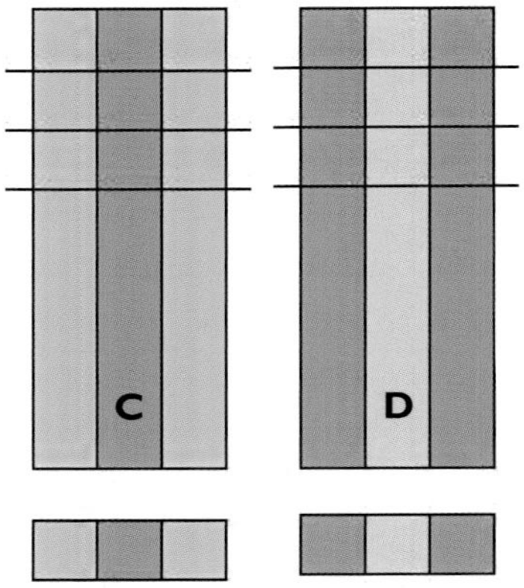


Sew segments together to make a nine-patch block as shown. Press seams to outer segments using a light spray starch. Repeat to make 27 Block B. Set blocks aside.

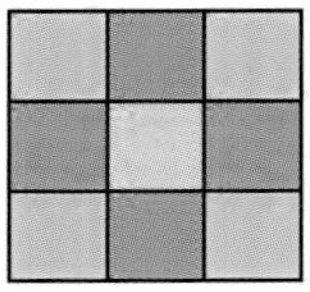

*Block B*

### MAKING X-BLOCKS

Place the X-Blocks tool on a nine-patch block, matching the solid lines of the tool to the seams of the block. Carefully cut along the edges of the X-Blocks with a rotary cutter. Set aside the X-tra's for your border. Cut all Block A and Block B in this manner.

Place blocks into separate stacks; Block A and Block B.

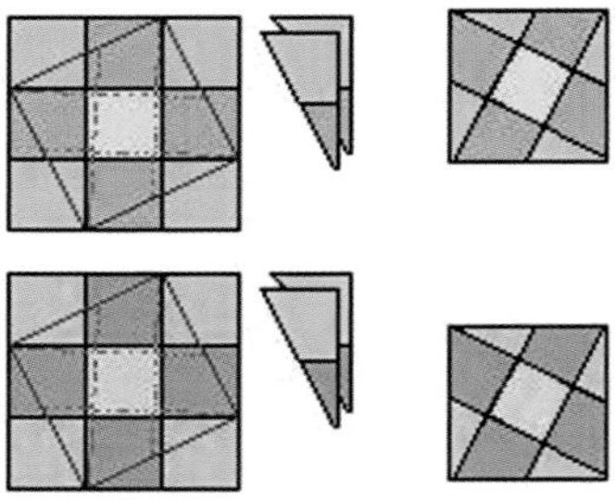

Remember - the edges of your cut block are bias. Handle your blocks gently after you cut them!

*Note: If you are using the Mini or Bellybutton X-Blocks, the X-tra's are very small and difficult to work with. You may just want to use a border of complementary fabric.*

# My Little Princess

## MAKING THE APPLIQUE PANEL

Trace the patterns on page 39 and refer to "Fusible-Web Applique" on page 9 to make the appliques from fabric specified in Materials list. If you are making this quilt with either the Mini or Bellybutton X-Blocks, you will need to reduce the appliqué shapes on page 39 to fit panel size. Arrange the applique shapes on the green panel strip as shown, placing swirls first, then adding flowers and dots as desired. Follow manufacturers' instructions to fuse the appliques in place. Machine stitch around edges of shapes to secure them in place.

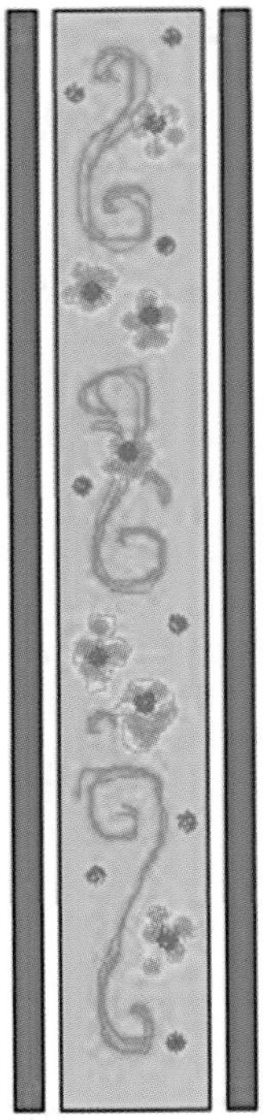

Sew two aqua strips together end to end to make one long strip. Repeat with the two remaining strips. (Skip this step if making the Mini or Bellybutton size). Sew the strips to the long edges of the appliquéd panel. Press seams to the aqua strips.

## ASSEMBLING THE QUILT TOP

### Block Section 1

Sew 18 each Block A and Block B together into 9 rows of 4 blocks each, alternating Block A and Block B in each row. Press seams toward Block B. Sew the rows together. Press seams in either direction.

### Block Section 2

Sew 9 Block A and Block B together into 9 rows of 2 blocks each, alternating Block A and Block B in each row. Press seam allowances toward Block B. Sew rows together. Press seams in either direction, or open.

Sew Block Sections 1 and 2 to the long edges of the appliquéd panel as shown. Press seams toward the aqua strips.

## ADDING X-TRA'S SIDE BORDERS

Sew X-tra's from Block A and Block B together as shown in diagram to make a rectangle. Repeat with all X-tra's. Trim all rectangles to an equal size. (This size will vary depending on X-Blocks tool used, individual seam allowance, etc.)

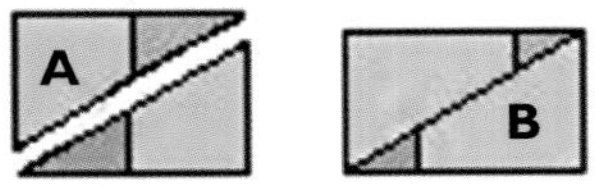


Measure the sides of the quilt top. Sew long sides of rectangles together as shown to fit measurement, alternating pink and blue points every 4th rectangle. Repeat for opposite side. Sew X-tra border to each side of quilt top; press seams to quilt top.

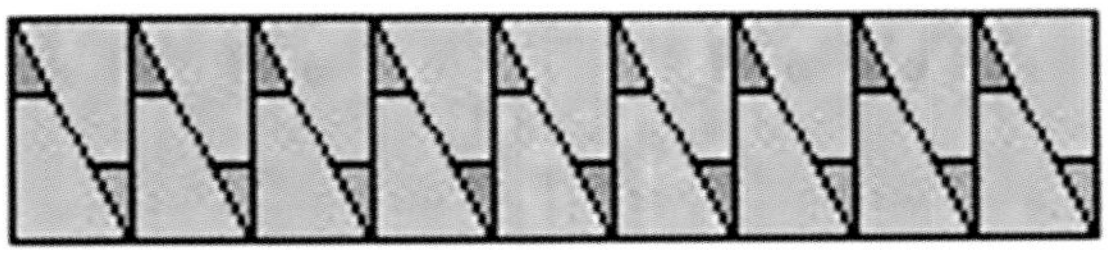

# My Little Princess

Refer to "Happy Endings" on page 8 to trim out the floral border strips to the lengths needed for the outer border and sew them to the quilt top. Press seam allowances toward the border.

### FINISHING THE QUILT

Refer to "Happy Endings" on page 8 to layer and baste your quilt, and quilt as desired. Prepare binding and sew it to the quilt edges.

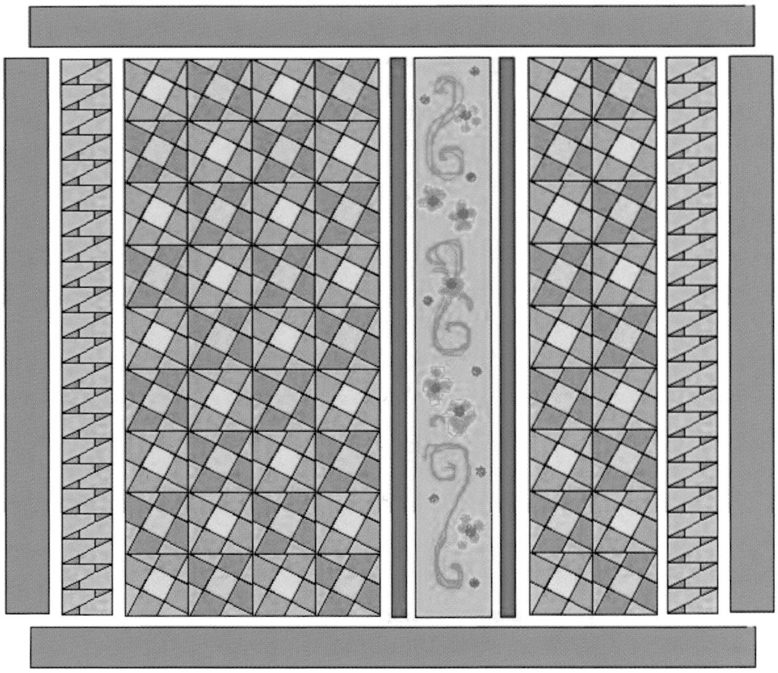

*Quilt Assembly*

# Happily Ever Laughter

*...Laughter is the music of the heart*

Quilt made by Patricia Pepe

# Crown Jewels

*...Treat every day as a gift and treasure it for itself*

Quilt made by Rebecca True

# Materials

Yardages are based on 42"- wide fabrics

| Finished quilt size | 75" x 89" | 66" x 78" | 34" x 41" - 30" x 36" | 32" x 41" - 28" x 34" |
|---|---|---|---|---|
| | **7½" X-Blocks** | **6½" X-Blocks** | **Mini-7.5 Mini-6.5** | **Bellybutton-7.5 Bellybutton-6.5** |
| Asst. medium to dark teal & copper prints | 5¼ yds. | 4 yds. | 1¾ yd. | 1½ yds. |
| Asst. light & neutral prints | 2¾ yds. | 2 yds. | 1 yd. | ¾ yd. |
| Light background | 1½ yd. | 1¼ yd. | n/a | n/a |
| Copper mottle solid for border | 1¾ yd. | 1¼ yd. | ½ yd. | ⅓ yd. |
| Dark red solid for inner border | ⅓ yd. | ⅓ yd. | ¼ yd. | ¼ yd. |
| Binding | ¾ yd. | ¾ yd. | ½ yd. | ½ yd. |
| Backing | 6 yds. | 5 yds. | 1 yd. | 1 yd. |

# Cutting Chart

Cut all strips across the width of the fabric (WOF) - 42"- 44"

| | **7½" X-Blocks** | **6½" X-Blocks** | **Mini-7.5 X-Blocks** | **Mini-6.5 X-Blocks** | **Bellybutton - 7.5 X-Blocks** | **Bellybutton - 6.5 X-Blocks** |
|---|---|---|---|---|---|---|
| Med. to dark teal & copper prints | 48 strips - 3¾" | 42 strips - 3¼" | 27 strips - 2⅛" | 24 strips - 1⅞" | 24 strips - 2" | 21 strips - 1¾" |
| Light neutral prints | 24 strips - 3¾" | 21 strips - 3¼" | 15 strips - 2⅛" | 12 strips - 1⅞" | 12 strips - 2" | 12 strips - 1¾" |
| Light background | 7 strips - 6½" | 6 strips 5½" | n/a | n/a | n/a | n/a |
| Copper mottle solid | 12 strips - 4"<br>5 strips - 1½" | 8 strips - 3¾"<br>4 strips - 1½" | 4 strips - 3" | 3 strips - 3" | 3 strips - 3" | 3 strips - 3" |
| Dark red solid for inner border | 7 strips - 1½" | 6 strips - 1½" | 3 strips - 1" | 3 strips - 1" | 3 strips - 1" | 3 strips - 1" |
| Binding | 8 strips 2¼" | 7 strips 2¼" | 5 strips 2¼" | 4 strips 2¼" | 5 strips 2¼" | 4 strips 2¼" |

# Segment Cutting Chart

Cut segments after sewing into strip sets per instructions

| | **7½" X-Blocks** | **6½" X-Blocks** | **Mini-7.5 X-Blocks** | **Mini-6.5 X-Blocks** | **Bellybutton - 7.5 X-Blocks** | **Bellybutton - 6.5 X-Blocks** |
|---|---|---|---|---|---|---|
| Cut all strip segments | 3¾" | 3¼" | 2⅛" | 1⅞" | 2" | 1¾" |

# Crown Jewels

## MAKING THE BLOCKS

Sew 3 different medium/dark strips together to make medium strip set. Press seams to center strip. Repeat with all medium/dark strips, rearranging the placement of fabrics in each strip set.

Sew 3 different light strips together to make light strip set. Press seams to outside strips. Repeat with all light strips, changing the placement of fabrics in each strip set.

Referring to Segment Cutting Chart for measurement, cut medium/dark strip sets into a total of 160 segments and light strip sets into a total of 80 segments.

**Make sure to double check the measurement for the size X-Blocks tool you are using!**

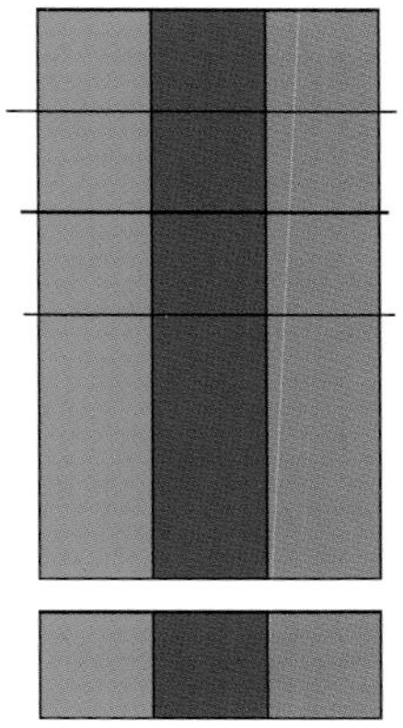

*Medium/Dark Strip Set*
*Cut 160 segments*

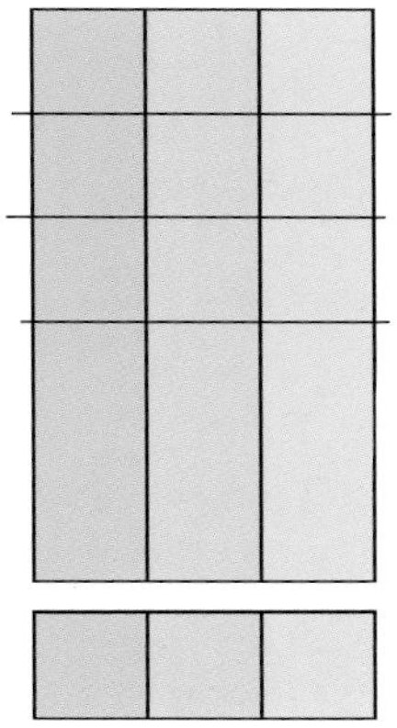

*Light Strip Set*
*Cut 80 segments*

Sew segments together to make nine-patch blocks as shown, always placing the light segments between two medium segments. Using a light spray starch, press seams to outer segments on 40 blocks. On the remaining 40 blocks, press seams with light spray starch toward the center segments. Keep blocks in two separate stacks of 40 blocks each.

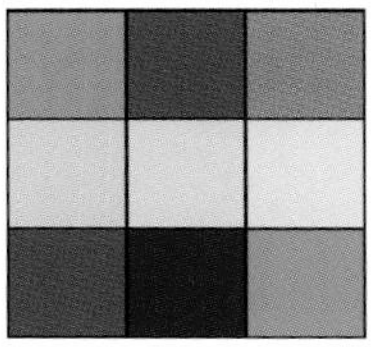

## BASIC X-BLOCKS

With the first stack, place the X-Blocks tool on a block, matching seams of block to solid lines of X-Blocks. Cut around the edges of the tool with a rotary cutter; set aside the cut-off (X-tra's). Repeat with all 40 blocks in the first stack.

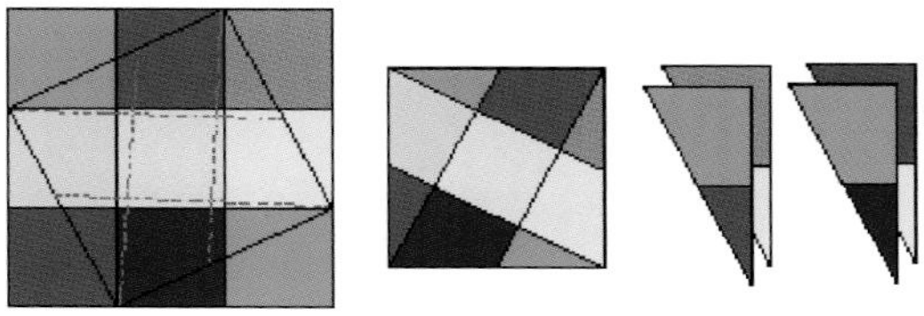

## REVERSE X-BLOCKS

Now, flip the X-Blocks tool over (the printed words on the tool will appear backward). Place the flipped X-Blocks tool on a nine-patch from the second stack, matching seams of block to solid lines of X-Blocks. Cut around the edges of the tool with a rotary cutter; set aside the X-tra's. Repeat with all 40 blocks in the second stack.

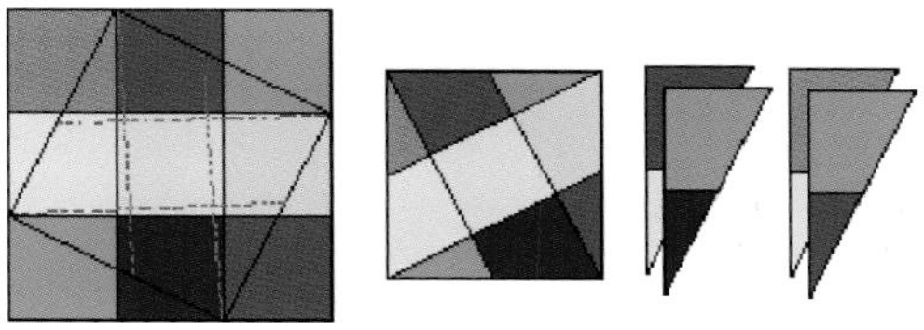

*Note: The X-tra's from the Mini & Bellybutton X-Blocks are small and difficult to work with. Use strips of copper and background to make borders.*

## QUILT TOP ASSEMBLY

Following diagram carefully, sew blocks together into 10 rows of 8 blocks each, alternating basic and reverse blocks in each row, placing the medium fabrics together to create diamonds. The light segments will create a zigzag. Press seams in opposite directions.

# Crown Jewels

If you have the advantage of using a design wall, it is very helpful to place the blocks on it as you cut them, referring to the quilt layout diagram for placement. This eliminates unnecessary handling of the blocks and helps visualize the design. Stand back a few feet to check placement of your blocks.

Sew the red inner border strips together end to end and press seam allowances to one side. Measure the quilt through the center from top to bottom and cut two border strips to that measurement. Sew to sides of quilt, press seams to quilt top. Repeat to add borders to top and bottom of quilt.

### ADDING THE X-TRA OUTER BORDER

Measure the width and length of an X-tra (cut-off). Cut 64 rectangles from background fabric strips this measurement. Cut half of the background rectangles on the diagonal from top left to bottom right; cut remaining rectangles on diagonal from top right to bottom left as shown in diagram to make triangles the same size as your X-tra's;.

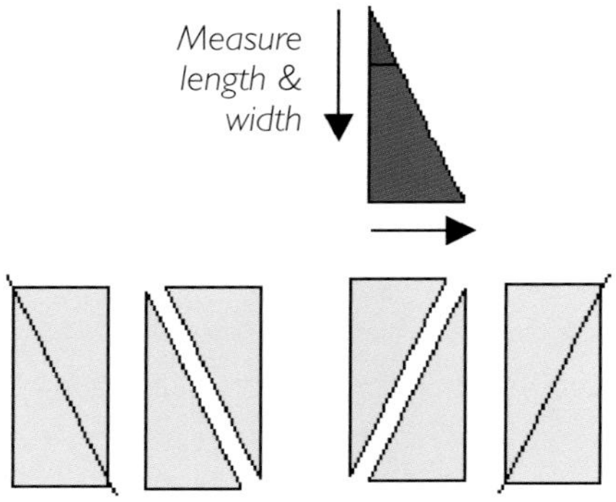


*Cut background rectangles*

Sew the X-tra's from both the basic and reverse X-Blocks to a corresponding background triangle as shown below to make rectangles. Trim all rectangles to an equal size. (This will vary depending on X-Blocks tool used, individual seam allowance, seam off-set, etc.)

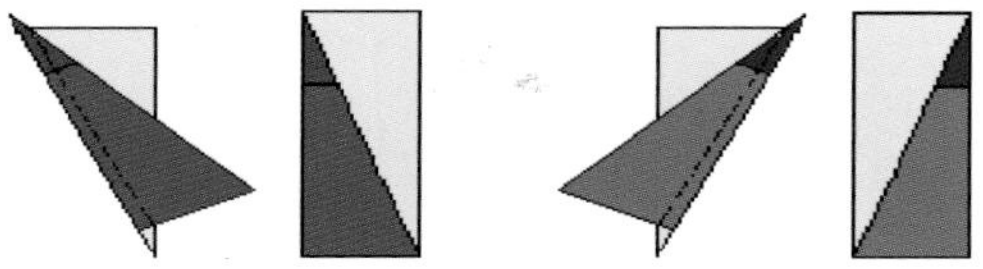

Sew 2 basic and 2 reverse rectangles together as shown to create diamonds, using a 3/8" – 1/2" seam in center. Repeat to make 32 diamonds.

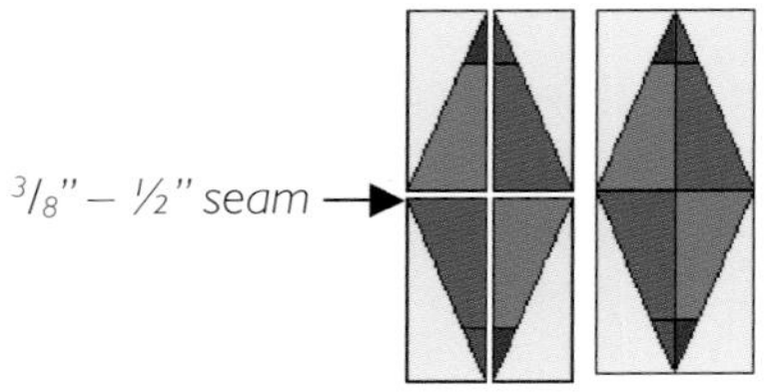


Sew narrow copper strip to each end of 12 diamonds. Press seams to copper strip.

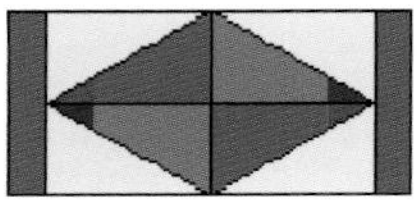

Sew wide copper strips to long sides of 20 diamonds. Trim these so the width is the same as the length of the copper end diamonds.

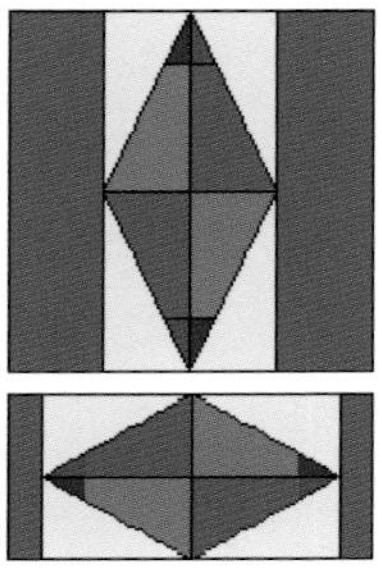

Sew 4 copper-side diamonds and 3 copper-end diamonds together as shown to make top border. Repeat for bottom border. Measure quilt through the center from side to side. Add copper and background strips to border if necessary to fit this measurement. Sew diamond border to top and bottom of quilt.

**Magic Rotary Cutter Wand TIP**

**Before you start, test your seam allowance by sewing a sample strip set. Place the X-Blocks tool on the strip set and make sure the seams line up with the lines on the X-Blocks. Adjust seam allowance if necessary.**

# Crown Jewels

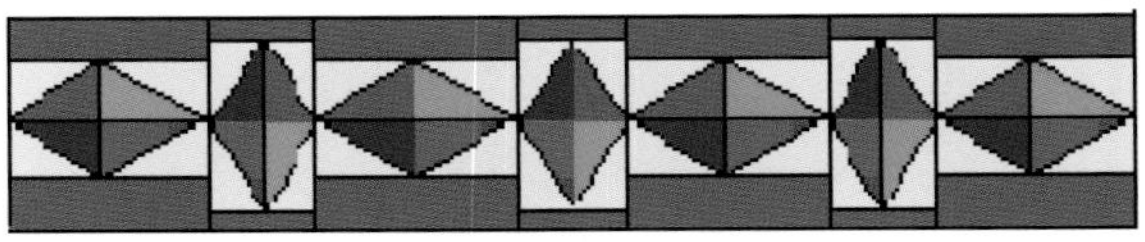

Sew 6 copper-side and 3 copper-end diamonds together as shown in quilt assembly diagram for side borders. Sew wide copper strip to one end of background strip as shown. Cut this to the same width as the border. Repeat to make a total of 4. Referring to diagram, add copper strip to end of border strips.

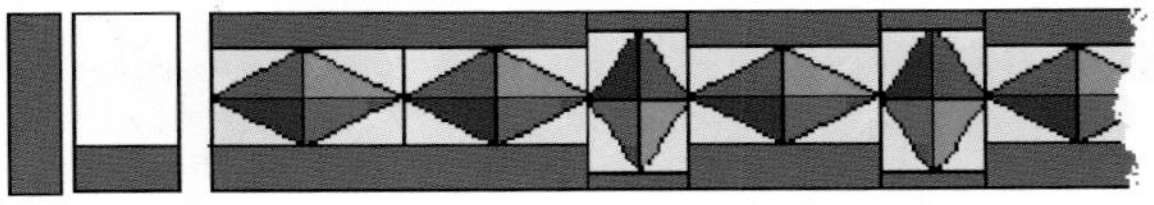

Sew to the sides of the quilt, press seam allowances toward the inner border.

### FINISHING THE QUILT

Refer to "Happy Endings" on page 8 to layer and baste your quilt; quilt as desired. Prepare binding strips and sew to quilt.

*Quilt Assembly*

# Coloring Play Pens©
# Basic X-Blocks

# Coloring Play Pens©
# Reverse X-Blocks

**The Queen grants you permission to copy this page**

Soli Deo Gloria